# THE NOT-SO-WILD CLOSED SYLLABLE EXCEPTIONS

# PHONICS READ-ALOUDS

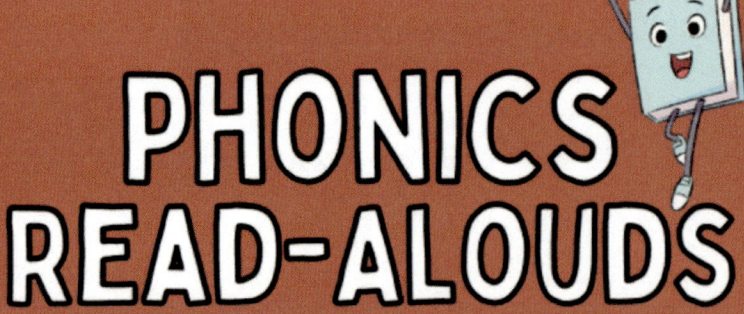

Title: The Not-So-Wild Closed Syllable Exceptions
ISBN: 9798311557252
First Published in the United States of America, 2025

Contributors: Manns, Yvette, author; Blu, Ana K., illustrator

Summary: W ventures out west to capture the closed syllable exceptions. When he brings them to meet his letter friends, he discovers that these "rulebreakers" serve a helpful role in building new words.

This is an original work fiction. Any references to historical events, real people or real places are used fictitiously. Names, characters, concepts, places, events are imaginative ideas and any resemblance to actual people, ideas, places are coincidental.

www.PhonicsReadAlouds.com

# THE NOT-SO-WILD CLOSED SYLLABLE EXCEPTIONS

Written by: Yvette Manns
Illustrated by: Ana K. Blu

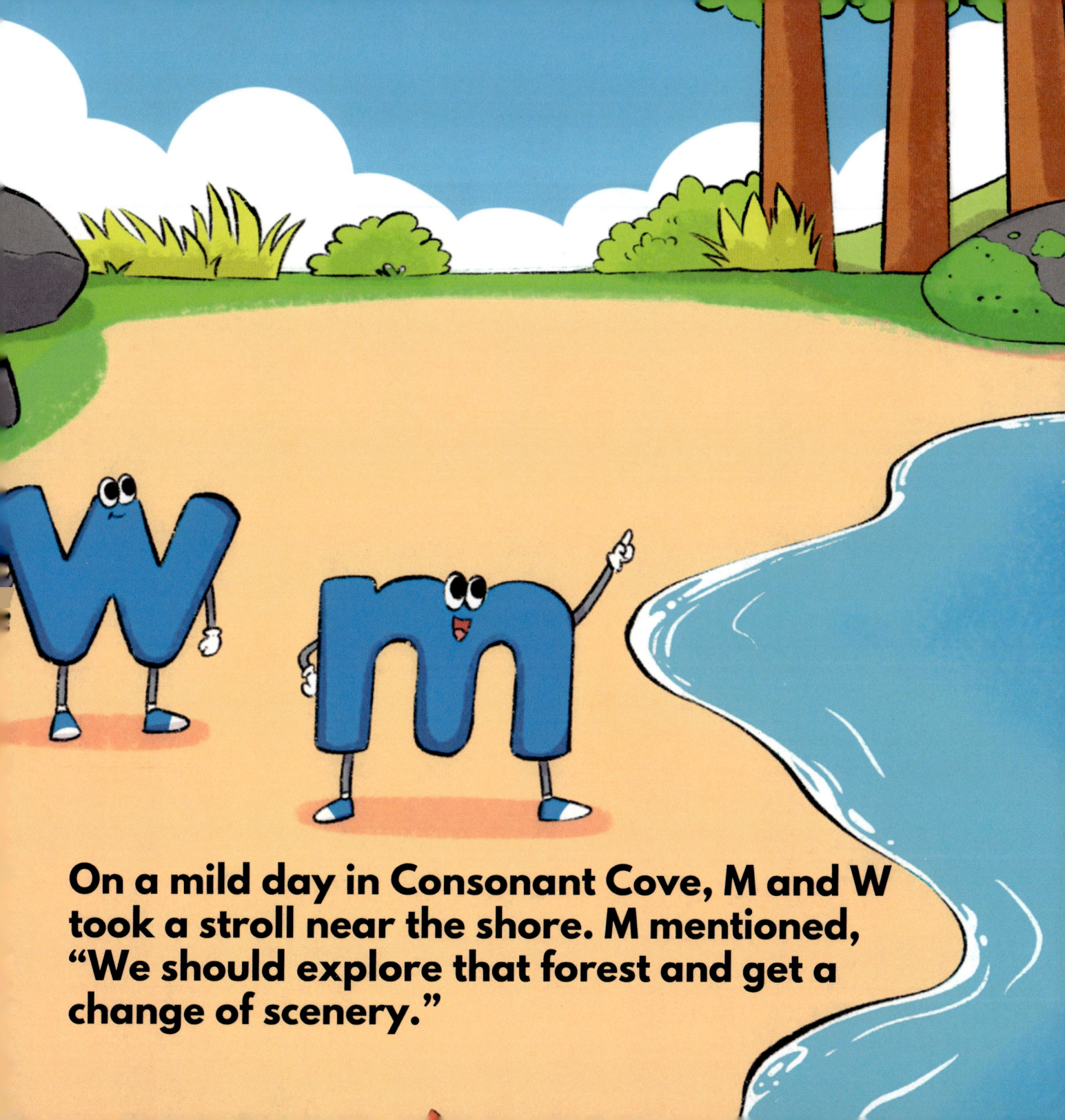

**On a mild day in Consonant Cove, M and W took a stroll near the shore. M mentioned, "We should explore that forest and get a change of scenery."**

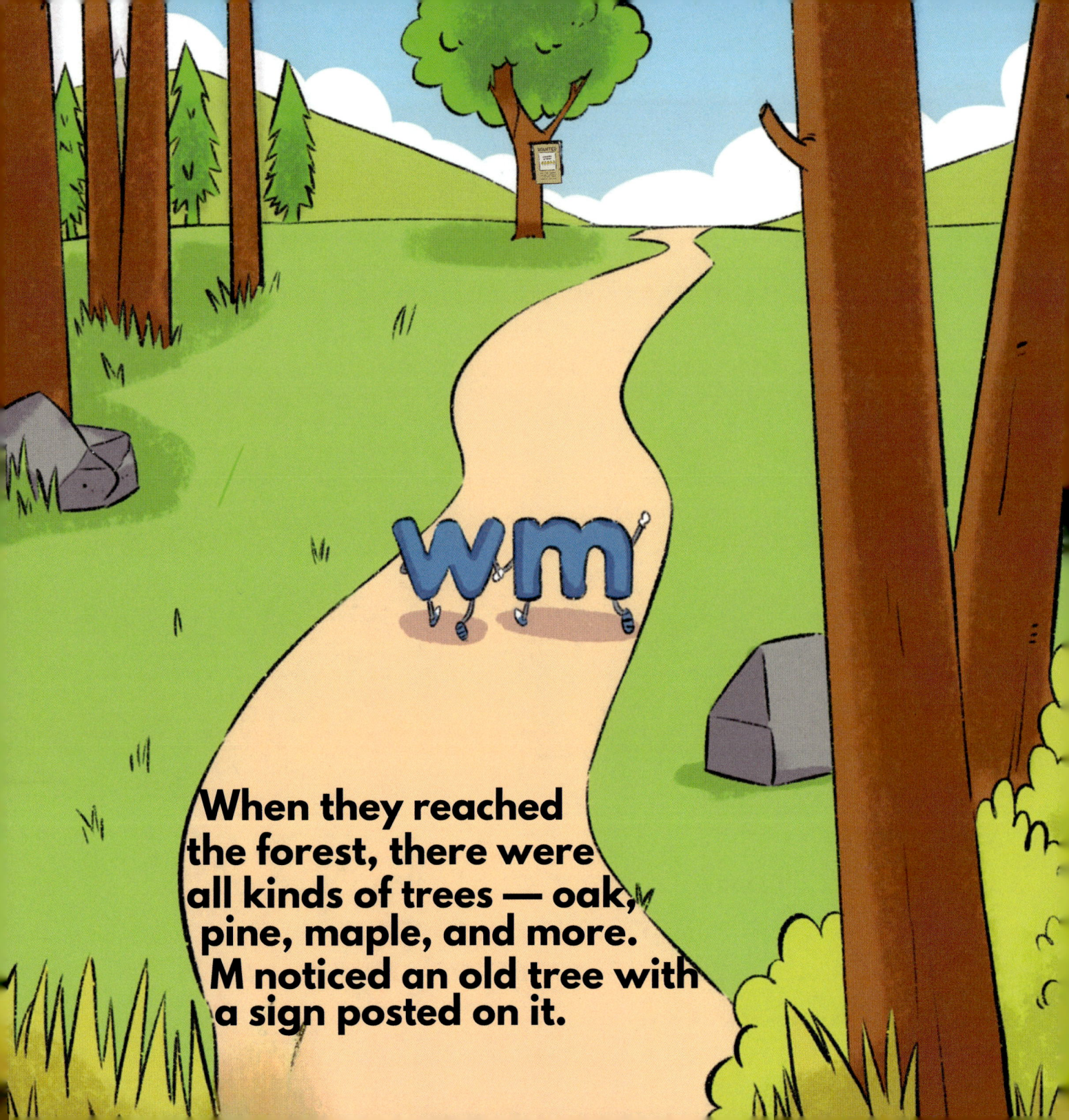

When they reached the forest, there were all kinds of trees — oak, pine, maple, and more. M noticed an old tree with a sign posted on it.

W read the sign aloud. "Wanted: Wild Letters on the Run. Reward - $1,000 in Gold Coins." He yanked the sign off the tree and said, "I know what needs to be done."

W left and got Bolt, his trusty colt, from his horse stable. This young horse got his name because he could gallop at the speed of lightning, and when he stopped, he'd stand up on his hind legs.

Determined to find the wild letters, W rode Bolt out west. He brought the sign with him to remind himself of what these groups of letters looked like so he could easily find them.

Out west, the townspeople were nowhere to be found. W finally located the town's sheriff hiding behind the door at his station.
"Sheriff," W declared. "I am here to capture the wild letters and claim the gold."

The sheriff replied, "Please help us! Those letters are out of control. I must remind you, they are very wild. Most people haven't been able to get a hold of them."

W told him, "Well, Sheriff, I'm not most people. Those letters need to learn to follow the rules." W rode off on his colt.

At high noon, W heard a commotion from the town square. The wild letters were wreaking havoc! -ild took candy from a child, -ost made ghost noises to scare people, and -old, -olt, and -ind got into all kinds of mischief!

Bolt let out a loud snort and stomped his hooves. The wild letters stopped their chaos with a jolt. -ind said, "We don't take too kindly to strangers around these parts. Who are you and why are you here?" W answered, "I'm here to teach you to mind your manners and behave like letters should."

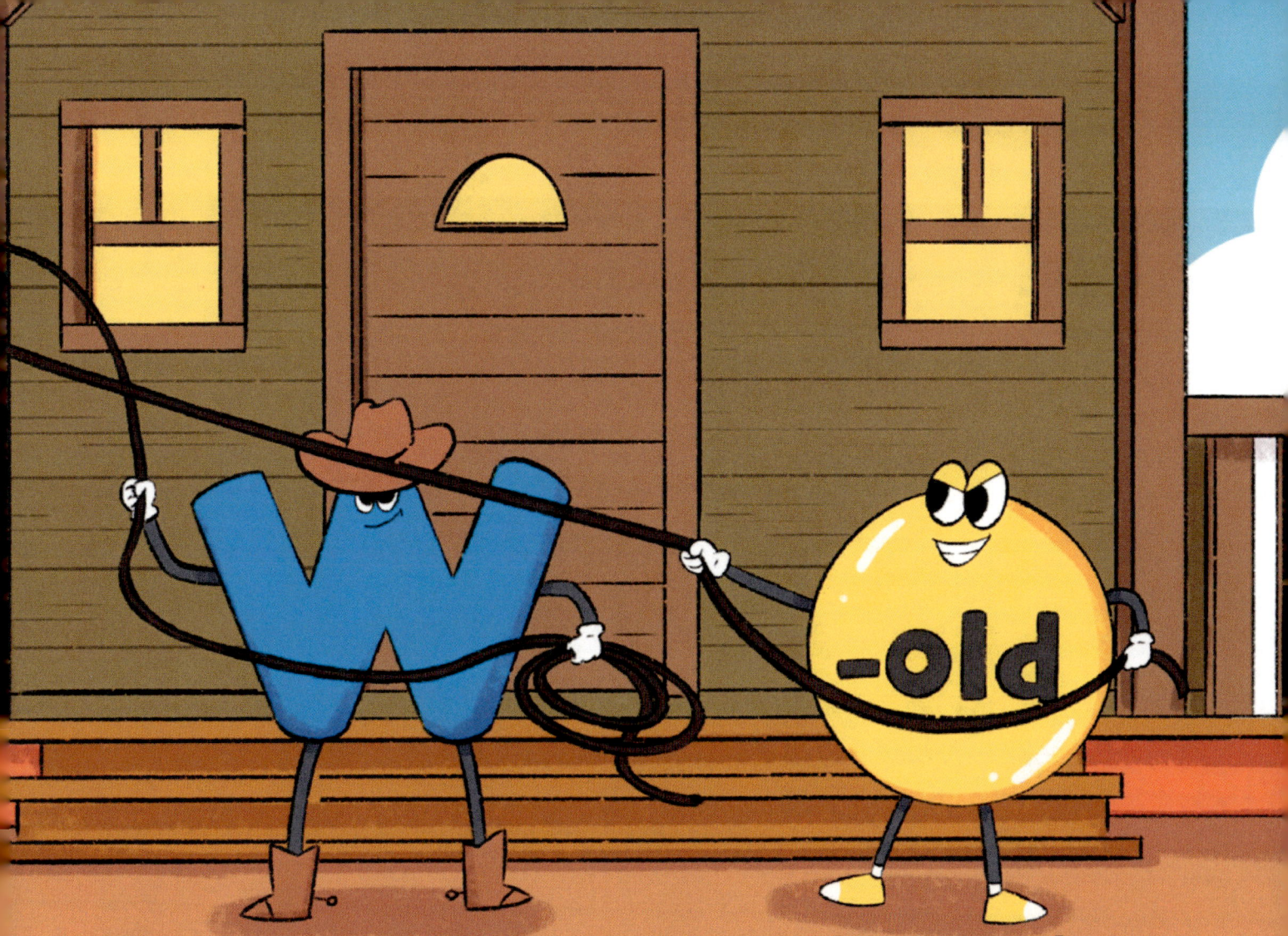

With a twirl of his lasso, W spun his rope above his head to wind the letters up. Suddenly, the wild letters yanked his lasso out his hand to bind him up instead! "That was mighty bold of you," -old told W. The wild letters carried W and Bolt away to hold them in their saloon.

Desperate to be freed, W reasoned with the wild letters. "If you let us go, I'll show you how other letters behave and work together to build words, instead of running wild. The letters back in Consonant Cove and Vowel Valley follow the rules and get along with everyone."

**The wild letters agreed and they arrived just as the consonants and vowels were preparing to build words. L said, "Welcome! Let me explain how we work together to build words."**

L continued, "When we build words, we know that the vowel is usually short in a closed syllable or a word when it ends with a consonant, such as lap and milk. Since English is made of many languages and patterns, there are some words that don't follow the rules."

-old boldly stated, "Good, because we don't like rules. We are the exception to the rules." M remarked, "Wait! That just gave me an idea about how the closed syllable exceptions can help us." M showed -old how they could build the word "mold."

mold

-ost said, "Building a word looks kind of fun." -ild, -ind, -old, and -olt chimed in, "Let's create some words, too!"

The closed syllable exceptions worked with the consonants to form the words "post," "mild," "bind," "cold," and "volt."

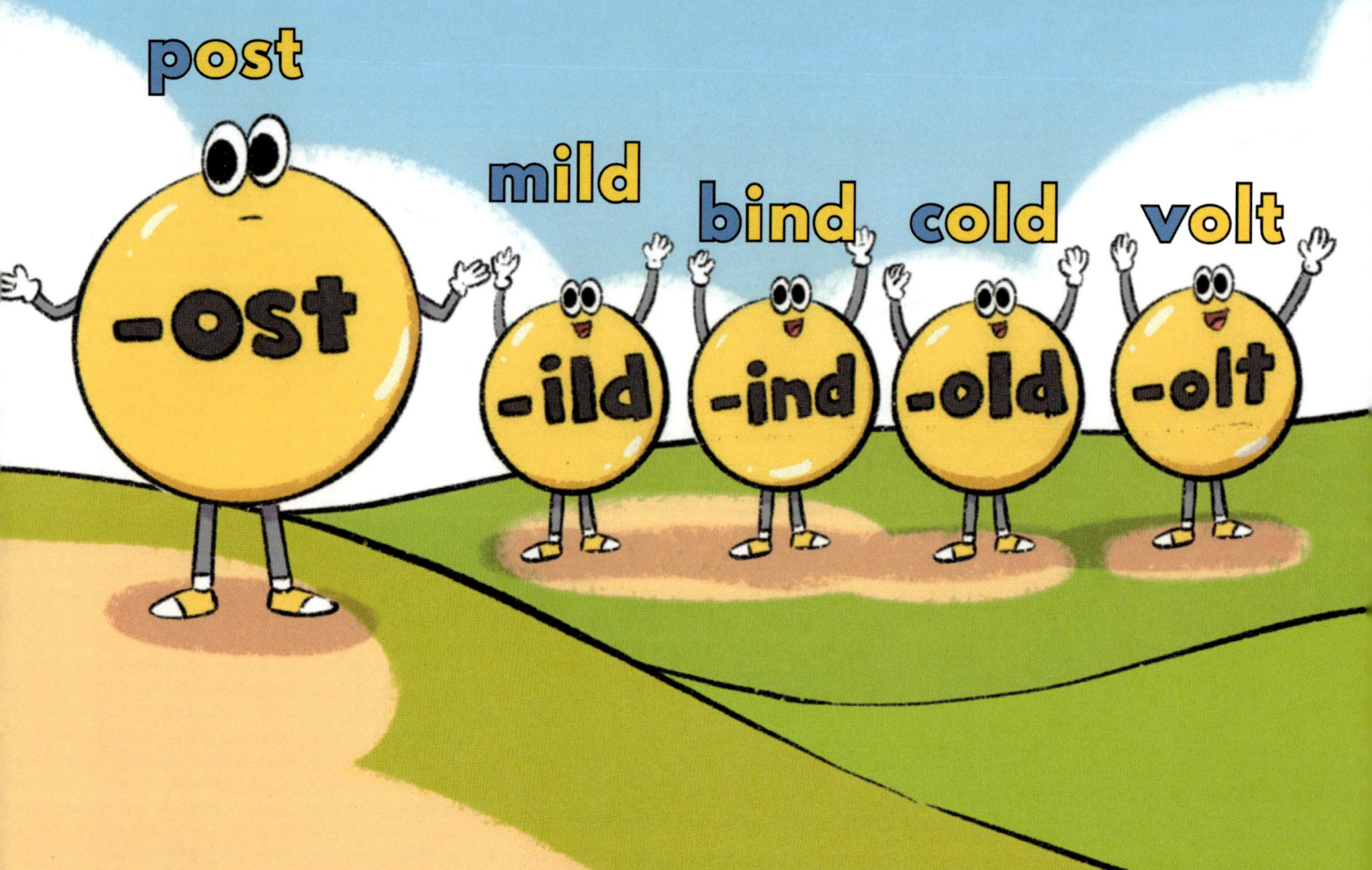

-ind answered, "I can help when you are building the word that means 'to turn.' I, N, and D can help when you are building the word that means 'breeze.' There are also some words that look like us, like 'cost' and frost,' but they are just regular closed syllables."

"Well, Closed Syllable Exceptions," W said. "It turns out that your rule-breaking behavior is actually helpful at times. Before I take you back out west to get my gold, let's make a deal. Promise that you won't be so wild around town. If so, you can return here and we will host you again. How does that sound?"

# "WE'RE SOLD"

they shouted.

# TIPS FOR AFTER READING

- Go on a word hunt and list all the words in this story with closed syllable exceptions.
- Sort the words you find by the closed syllable exception pattern and share with a classmate.
- Read all the words with closed syllable exceptions out loud.
- Draw the wild letters and list as many closed syllable exceptions as you can.
- Using another passage or text, highlight all the words with closed syllable exceptions that you can find.

# FUN FACTS ABOUT CLOSED SYLLABLE EXCEPTIONS

- Closed syllable exceptions are words that look like they should have a short vowel sound because they end with a consonant sound, but the vowel sound is long.
- Words that end with -ild, -ind, -old, -olt and -ost are usually closed syllable exception words.
- There are a few words that don't fit this pattern such as: lost, build and frost.
- The word "wind" can be a closed syllable word and a closed syllable exception word. One version of the word means a breeze and the other version means to turn or spin.
- Sometimes, these words are called, "Wild Old Colt Words," "Rulebreakers" or "CVCC Exceptions."
- Here are some more words that end with closed syllable exceptions:

bold  child  colt  find  fold  ghost  golden  grind
host  kind  mild  post  remind  scold  told  wild

CAN YOU THINK OF ANY MORE WORDS WITH CLOSED SYLLABLE EXCEPTIONS?

# CHECK OUT OTHER BOOKS IN THE SERIES!

  ...and more books!

# STAY IN THE KNOW!

Visit
www.PhonicsReadAlouds.com
for activities, stickers, and more!

# DID YOU ENJOY THIS STORY?

Please consider leaving us a review on Amazon. This helps us to learn what you want to read about next and tell other people about our stories!

 **PhonicsReadAlouds**   **PhonicsReadAlouds**   **PhonicsReadAlouds**

Made in the USA
Coppell, TX
16 July 2025